Moonbroch

Naveena Bhashini

NOEL LORENZ HOUSE OF FICTION

Kolkata   Haflong

Noel Lorenz House of Fiction
Headquarters - Kolkata, West Bengal, India
154A, KCG Road, Kolkata - 700050
www.noellorenz.com

Naveena Bhashini

❥ ❥ ❥ ❥

Naveena Bhashini

From: Neyveli, India

Instagram: its_bhashy_here

Acknowledgement

I want to thank Almighty for all his grace throughout.

I also thank NLHF for giving me a chance to publish this book.

Special thanks to my family (momma and dad) and brother Nihithan Ken for being a pillar of support.

There are many more people I could thank, but time, space and modesty compel me to stop here.

Naveena Bhashini

About the Author

Naveena Bhashini is new budding author, poet and creative writer.

She is from Neyveli-the lignite city.

She has completed B. Tech in biotechnology stream and currently working as a corporate professional.

She is well versed in writing fun, sweet, love and motivational packed creative writings.

She loves to express her emotions and she wants to treasure her feelings through words.

She believes that nothing is much more joy than her writings touch other's heart, she wants her writings should travel within the reader's mind and heart.

Naveena Bhashini

Her characters are clever and fearless in real life and in word she has constant to her saying let me face it.

She is bold and straightforward which is her best behavior and a going with the flow person.

She never worries about the past and don't think too much about the future.

Naveena is best known for her short glimpse of the poems and currently working to achieve her dream to be an author known to the world.

Sharing her mind through pen and paper for connecting peoples with her words.

Naveena Bhashini

About the Book

This is my first book which was my dream come true, feels like happened in a single night. This book will definitely motivate you in all directions of your life. Life is not on same style for everyone, you will feel your life is the hardest one until you hear some other's story. Life is always being on its own way neither or nor beyond our imaginations.

Life should be considered as a New Page in a book. It's always a new hope looking at the blank page, where I can create my very own path which leads to my way home to dream. It's also a fresh kick start, where I can start new without any regret, I can also erase the old errors. I can edit or even re-edit my new page, a small dot can be seen unique and larger, when it is on the

Naveena Bhashini

blank page... As like a tiny step I'm taking forward, may be a greater one when I look back, after a mile crossed.

Naveena Bhashini

A Collection of Poetry

Naveena Bhashini

Contents

Naveena Bhashini

Naveena Bhashini

When love happens

When love happens

I felt like I have achieved something greater,

As it is not easy to find a soulmate

Who is perfect to my soul and mind.

Because he should be the better version of me

In handling my bad attitude when I am not myself.

No matter what, I should be his first most priority

Vice-versa he is to me.

We should share our whole day's experience to each

Other at the day end.

Happy that I have that kinda man in my life,

Who have never failed to be that

One perfect man.

Your name reminds me

The happy moments, we have spent together

The effort, you took to make me stay

The cheering smile, you had to boost me

The hand, which is always there to pat my shoulder

The energy, you always showed up to motivate me

When I am down.

Even when you are hundreds of miles far,

Your name can make me smile enough.

Naveena Bhashini

Nights are not for

Nights are not for,

Just worrying and bringing up

All trashes to mind.

Nights are not for,

Throwing away sleep and tiring the eyes.

Nights are not for,

Regretting things that you have

Done in the past.

Nights are not for,

Predicting your future,

Which is useless.

Because, life surprises us

With new experience everyday.

Nights are for thanking god

Naveena Bhashini

For he made us breath till.

Nights are for thanking yourself

*For you have completed your day
successfully*

Without giving up.

*Nights are for thanking your
supporters and haters,*

For they pushed us to run more.

Nights are for appreciating your body

*For it didn't stop working the whole
day,*

And so it should be rewarded with

GOOD SLEEP...!

Naveena Bhashini

Hope

I keep my windows open

Because,

Sometimes when I'm drowned in

Full of fears,

Full of hopelessness,

Full of drought,

Full of emotions,

That small light wave

Sprinkled through the small wholes

Of the windows.

Teaches me big lessons.

Its shows me that even little hope

Can bring me up.

Hope has super power,

Naveena Bhashini

Which can even bright up a person

Who is at his last chance to live

By making a way.

Life without hope is like

Sleepwalking (somnambulism)

Because you will never know

What has been kept before you,

Even your eyes are opened....!

Naveena Bhashini

What love means

I love you is not my feelings for you...

It is my heart beat rhythm.

It sings melancholic when you are far

It sings melody while watching you sleeping

It sings rap when you are close to my heart

And sometimes it sings a new song,

Which is repeating your name...!

For me, your notifications are

Switches that has control over my moods,

Literally it can change my gloomy face to

Ear reaching smile...

Naveena Bhashini

For me, your notifications are
Strings of bell that is
Directly connected to the heart,
Making my heart flash brightly...
I am surprised in love,
How can I deserve someone like you.
It is you, who made me ask myself,
Do I really worth him...?
By the way you treat me.

Naveena Bhashini

Let's have dinner

Come sit by my side,

My ears are eagerly waiting

To hear your whole day story,

I am ready to catch your feelings

Through your eyes.

Spit all your hidden emotions

You are carrying behind your mind,

Let me be your mirror,

You are always welcome

To vent your anger on your mirror.

I'll give you the fullest hope

To trust me completely.

So that you don't need to hide anything,

Naveena Bhashini

*Instead sharing all your secrets with
me.*

Believe me, I won't bring it up again

Which you don't want to hear.

Let me be the running water,

You can throw up all your worries

Like throwing up stones in the water.

It won't come back,

Reminding you the old things again.

Once you are ease at mind,

Let's have our dinner...

Naveena Bhashini

Holding relationship

I was holding our relationship like

The black cloud holds the rain...

Even though it is heavy and I can't hold more

I don't want to widened my hand to release you...

Even though I was hit by a strong wind,

I tried harder to hold you tight.

Thunder doesn't stop disturbing me,

It frightened me like hell.

But I never realized that it is a warning.

I got to know the truth so late...

That holding you long will hurt me more,

Naveena Bhashini

When you want to leave my hands...

*Finally, you got out of my hands
willingly,*

When I can't stop you back...

Alright..!

*I'm happy now with the burden free
hands...*

*Playing long with the winds and
thunders*

That doesn't mean to hurt me...

But they are the guarding angels

Holding me secretly...

Naveena Bhashini

Those who make u cry

Those who make you cry

Doesn't know how deep the stone reaches

When they throw it on the river.

*It makes them happy throwing stones in the
water*

Enjoying watching stones disturbing the layer.

But they won't imagine what is the reaction that

Actually happens under water.

*They don't know that they are collapsing the
dust*

Which we have hidden in deep,

So that they can't hurt us any longer.

People are like stones

Some hide the dust,

Some triggers the dust.

Its all about,

Staying with the right people.!

Naveena Bhashini

Dream

Without dreams,

Life is just like a half painted art,

Which doesn't have the complete meaning...

If I had a control over my dreams,

I will always have you in my dream

My eyes will never be

Tired of watching you

I can see you for the whole day

I can also continue

Seeing you in my dreams.

You not only fill my eyes with joy

Also making my heart overflowing

Like a river,

Making my blood cells dance

Naveena Bhashini

And increasing my love hormones.

Why not will I stop

Having happiness in my heart...?

When seeing you is my

All time favorite job to do.

Naveena Bhashini

Heart searches

My heart often searches for

The old you...

Who cared me,

more than himself.

Who loved me,

more than anyone can do.

Who couldn't bear,

my sinked eyes.

Who couldn't hold his anger long,

if I am sad.

Who couldn't bear,

missing me.

Who would have my picture near,

while sleeping.

Who can travel long,

for a 5 minutes talk.

And who promised me that,

he wouldn't leave me...

Naveena Bhashini

Stress buster

All my stress disappears when

I looked up at you standing near me...

I am freezed for a moment

When I saw your bright eyes...

Which conveys me

Hundreds of positive notes.

And simple gazed smile

Where my eyes got strucked with.

Bit later when my conscious is back

I looked at your hands,

Holding a cup of coffee

Which you have especially

Prepared for me,

Knowing that I am stressed.

Naveena Bhashini

When eyes are wet,

I close my eyes to bring you

In my retina.

So that I'll smile for no reasons

And cry no more...

Naveena Bhashini

Space

Sometimes, love just needs

A space...

Where I can adapt to you...

When you are out showing the real you

Which you usually hide

From the world.

I can cover your eyes with love

That fills your heart with peace.

So that you can pour out yourself

And get back to the

Same as for you too,

*I may show smiling face all over the
day.*

But deep inside

I may have hidden emotions

Naveena Bhashini

Which inly you can tolerate,

And help me bring back

My real smile...!

Of course, you are the lawyer

Who always end our fights first.

You never cared being a looser

In our every argument.

May be I should agree,

That you are the reason for

Our relationship to grow on.

Naveena Bhashini

Dear moon

Dear Moon,

I know you love me secretly

Appearing at dark after I slept,

Hiding in the daytime

So that I can't question you...

I know you are sometimes worried

When you can't see me

And turned your face dull.

I know you sometimes cry along with me

And hiding you half face.

Naveena Bhashini

I know you are sometimes sick and disappear

When you are afraid of losing me…

Oh Moon….!

Naveena Bhashini

Weather is different

The weather is different

When I am close to your heart

Hearing your heartbeat

Resting my head in your shoulder

Holding you in my arms....!

Sometimes you really made me Feel like

I am somewhere out of this world.

Sometimes, You are taking me to fairy land

Making me fly high, along with my heart.

Sometimes, I feel like I am freezed

Even when the room is too hot.

Naveena Bhashini

*I never liked rainy days before you
came into my life,*

*But now, rainy days are the best
moments*

When you are with me.

*Enjoying the rain drops over the
window,*

Covered under single blanket,

Having coffee with some chit chats.

I want to leave

A strong impression in you

So that you can't forget me

Even if you have a memory loss.

Naveena Bhashini

Beauty of night

The beauty of night is

I hear your breath

Which sounds my name,

Loud and clear than in daytime.

Delighting the silent night,

Surrounded with millions of stars

Sprinkling love snow on the earth.

Nights are the day end,

That brings up many fights to end

By giving peaceful mind.

Moon and stars are the teachers

Teaching us about love.

*They proved that distance and time
doesn't*

Matter in love.

Naveena Bhashini

What decorates my night is
Covered under your arm,
Holding your fingers,
Hearing music through your
Breathing sound…!

Naveena Bhashini

Changes love brings

The change love brings,

Smile needs no reason,

Crying needs no time,

Never care day or night,

Doesn't bother mobile bills,

Long travel will not be tiresome,

Waiting long are not annoyed...

It feels like I am too worthy

To have a true love in life.

Love is not a gift

*Which is expensive and meant only for
some.*

Love is like an oxygen

*Which is everywhere, and much
needed to everyone*

Naveena Bhashini

But only few can feel it

And others just take it for granted.

Naveena Bhashini

Writer

*One who conveys his message
indirectly to someone,*

*One who imagine his own life with
fairy tales,*

*One who brings unimaginable things
in the paper,*

*One who exhibits his pain through
words,*

*One who doesn't matter money for his
words,*

*One who can change someone's mood
through his/her words,*

*One who cam give hope to some dying
soul,*

*One who can compare each other's
feelings.*

Writer has the power to create

Naveena Bhashini

Your IMAGINATIONS...

With the things that cannot be done in real

Which is far from your thinking

I can give u trust

Like miracle can happen suddenly

That you never dreamt for

Through my writings...!

Naveena Bhashini

I'm heartless since

I'm heartless since

The day I realized I have only me

When I needed someone to standby my side

When I realized my sacrifice for someone is unnoticed

When I haven't got a hand to raise me up

When my love for special one is doubted

When my care for someone is named as fake.

Someone I love once said to me:

Don't trust anyone so easily,

Or one day you will regret

For their true self...

Naveena Bhashini

I was too fool to recognize who is this
really belongs to...

Loneliness weighs heavy

When I am not really alone

Sitting corner of the room,

Burying my face under my arms.

But,

When I shut my mouth with fingers

Hiding my head under pillow covered
by blanket

And crying with no sound

When I am sleeping in the midst of
many.

Naveena Bhashini

If I write a book

If I write a book,

I'll dedicate it to the person

Who pushed me down

Who wanted to see me crying

Who tried hard to threw my happiness

Who enjoyed my darkest days

Who waited for my failure.

Some people are like books

Read and learn.

Take the good,

And leave the bad things

Along with the book.

The world outside is beautiful

Just widened your eyes,

Naveena Bhashini

It is all about how you see it.

If you have good thoughts,

Your way of seeing things

Will always be a positive thing.

Even stressing things can look like

Your external force

That takes you forward...!

Naveena Bhashini

I Never thought

I never thought,

A notification can make me smile.

I never thought,

A five minutes' conversation

Can change my mood.

I never thought,

Sleepless nights chats

Didn't make me tired.

I never thought,

Waiting wouldn't irritate me.

I never thought,

I will laugh looking at the wall.

I never thought,

Happiness doesn't need to come

Naveena Bhashini

From big things.

I never thought,

It will pain so much

When missing someone.

But all these were,

When the reason is YOU....!

Naveena Bhashini

If I were

If I were a mountain

I would stay still for all

Earthquakes and rains...

And strong enough,

That even you can't move me

Away from you...

If I were a lamp,

I would have accompanied you in all your dark nights,

I would have showed little light to boost your

hope in your bad days.

Those you were spending at darkest room,

Crying all alone.

To light a candle

Doesn't need to have a darkest surrounding.

You may not know someone's inner heart

Needs a light to bring up their hope.

Naveena Bhashini

One thing I appreciate

One thing I appreciate about my life is

It keeps me active...

*It pushes me down, after long try
when I got up*

It REPEATS...

I have become good at

*Reflecting my life as it goes so
smoothly*

As bed of roses...

Where actually it is so contradiction.

I often remind myself

That I am the role model for myself,

*I know my paths very well than
anyone can know...*

One good habit that made me

Naveena Bhashini

Who I am is

I don't turn back....!

We gain freedom

When we get to know

What others thinks of us

Is None of our business...

And start living as what we want to be...

When I am going with the flow

People think my morning starts with bliss

And my nights end in peace

Oh gosh....!

Naveena Bhashini

Thunder is good

Thunder is good, but

*Tearing for lot more times may
damage the sky...*

*Like thunders in life comes for
cleaning the dusted heart,*

*Throwing the trash apart and ends in
clearing path for forward march.*

*But frequent thunder may damage
heart*

Leading to lose hope...

In every situation,

I am getting a rebirth experience.

I'm hiding from the

Tears that will break me,

Thoughts that will take over me and

Naveena Bhashini

Expectations that will hurt me.

When people don't express themselves

They call it maturity...

But in real they are afraid of showing their

True nature,

And trying hard to play their,

Pseudo life role.

Life will become harsh when

You still want to hold it

Even after you know it is a thorn...!

Naveena Bhashini

Life is an ocean

Life is that ocean

Which has so many unique creatures

But remember,

You have your own style of living,

Because you are not the same,

Like the other creatures

You are crossing with.

Of course, it has heavy waves

And strong winds outside.

It is all about, how do you care

Your inner peace inside deep down.

You can never cross the ocean until

You haven't given up even after your wrestling

With multi storms and giant waves.

Naveena Bhashini

You will never change your life

Until you don't decide

To choose that one right road

Which can be your turning point...!

When life gives us two choices,

Never pick the one

Which feels smooth and easy...!

Because,

Good paths won't be easier...!

Naveena Bhashini

What makes life perfect

What makes life perfect

Is having you beside me

When I woke up in the morning

When I got you I realized that

All the great things are simple.

Your words mean that

I have so many reasons to live

And I am debted to

Live long with you...

Like the full moon

Though appearing once in a while

It is all time favorite to watch.

Likewise

My eyes can't stop admiring you

Naveena Bhashini

Everytime I see you

I have no words to explain

That how come you travelled so long

Just to spent a ten minutes with me.

Naveena Bhashini

What worth is

My biggest reward which really worth a lot for me is you,

Which I haven't imagine to have it for myself.

Love gives meaning to the millions of stars,

Starring at each other

Where no words are needed to be explained.

Just eyes can convey thousands of feelings....!

I wonder, how can you be this perfect

Giving me no chance to find a fault in you.

After your presence in my life,

Naveena Bhashini

I started believing that fairy tales are true,

I started believing true love exists,

I started believing magical miracle happens in life.

I keep getting older, stronger

And matured enough.

But my heart refuses,

It becomes so childish silly

And even more stupid

When I am with you....!

The weight of love will be found,

When you failed to measure your whole love...!

Because, love can only be immeasurable...!

If you can weigh it, then it can't be love...

Stars out fall for

Naveena Bhashini

Moon that is reflected in the water...!
Because, it knows which does
Really WORTH...!

Naveena Bhashini

Moon and the stars:

Till the stars don't shine

Sky is just an empty space.

Sky is meaningful only when,

The stars are stay hanging...

My life was empty,

Incomplete and meaningless.

Until you are in it.

But today,

Mu life worth to be the best book

Which has true words penned

With love and true feelings...!

There's a special thing about the moon

It triggers the heart by pumping out

Naveena Bhashini

Lovey-dovey butterflies...
It drenches me completely in love...!
So,
I fall in love little extra
With the person
Whom I'm watching
The moon with...!

When the world sleeps
The moon keeps admiring her loving sea
The same way I admire
Watching you sleeping.

Naveena Bhashini

Beauty

There is beauty in every woman

She is beautiful...!

with her bold eyes,

Which can even burn the enemies.

She is beautiful...!

with her confident walk

Which can take her to places that,

Others can't even imagine.

She is beautiful...!

with her strength and dignity

Which makes her stronger,

She can even move the mountain, that comes her way...!

Naveena Bhashini

Thoughts

Our thoughts reveal about

How capable we are...

Either positive towards all over situations

Or broken easily by taking up negative thoughts...

Burn those thoughts

Which are destroying the roots

Of your hearts.

Making you feel heavy and

At last causing death inside your soul...

Sometimes I would feel like

Saying to my mind that,

Naveena Bhashini

Dear overthinking,

Can you move out from me?

Your quarantine days are over...!

Sometimes I ask myself

Why should I worry...?

When my days on this earth

Is unpredictable.

Who can be so sure

That they will wake up

The next day morning...?

Our lives are as similar to the flowers,

It just takes a moment to wither

Even though it has already stayed strong

From wild winds...

Likewise,

Death is one thing

Naveena Bhashini

*Which is even god hasn't control over
it...*

Life is that song,

Which hurts when I was thinking

About the past.

The same song which motivates me

When I worried about my future.

The same song which boost my spirit

Saying forget the past.

My all-time mantra now is,

Stop worrying about the future

And start living the present moment

My life...

My lesson...

My experience...

Make me...

What I AM today...!

Naveena Bhashini

Superman

I am not surprised to hear that

Superman is real

Yes, he can carry al the burdens

Single handed and single headed

He has superpowers to make

My dream happens true.

He is strong enough to carry me

On his shoulder.

He is weak hearted too

When He cannot bear see me crying.

Superman still lives,

Not somewhere or far from my sight...

He is at my sight everyday

In my home...

My father, my strength...

Naveena Bhashini

I can't pay the debt,

That I am indebted to you...

I can only found the way

Of showing my extreme

Gratitude via these words...!

Naveena Bhashini

Oxytocin

My soul shivers when

I got drenched in your love rain...!

You'll always be the first one

To whom I rush

When I lack oxytocin

Your hugs increase,

My happy hormones...!

The time stood still when

I saw you rushing to the car

Running towards me again,

Bringing back an umbrella,

Holding upon my head,

Other hand grabbed my shoulder,

And taking me slowly back to the car.

Naveena Bhashini

All this was for a drizzle rain drop

Not a heavy but just begin to rain...

Oh man...what are you...!

You don't stop showing your care,

Even if it looked silly...

Naveena Bhashini

Waiting

Nothing affects me more,

Until when the most important

Person of my life

Walked across me like,

Passing by a stranger.

You are my sun,

I always thought that you are my sunshine,

Bring lights to my life.

If I were a sunflower

I do raise my neck

And don't take my eyes away

From the sun,

Even though it throws the wrath...

Naveena Bhashini

Like a candle

I'll keep shining out

And spreading light for you.

No matter how much I'm losing myself.

Love can be stupid

If it really gives you,

Whole hearted happiness.

Love follows those rules,

that grows from heart.

And not the one which arises from the mind.

Heart break isn't hard,

when it is shattered as pieces.

But it hurts the most

When I tried to join and fix the pieces

with a fake smile...!

Naveena Bhashini

My heart has a room,

and of course, it has doors

I'll keep open the doors for you

No matter how many times you leave

I still keep waiting for you....!

Naveena Bhashini

Thank you...!

Shouting to the world

Sharing my heartfelt joy,

That...

God has been so good to me.

He never stopped surprising me,

with his good deeds.

Grateful for all that I have now.

Even I can't believe that life is moving

Above cotton bed with roses.

Pinching myself to know,

if this is not a dream.

Being thankful is a two-way joy,

For both receiver and giver.

If I get a chance,

Naveena Bhashini

To stand on the world's top place

I'll hold the speaker,

Shouting loud all the names

Whom I want to thank.

I'll thank the persons,

Who made my life a meaningful one,

Who holded me when I fall,

Who lended me their hands to help me out,

And...

All those who came across my life...!

I thank you all...

For molding my character,

For making me bold,

For showing me who am I,

Who brought out my talents,

And who is there always

When I turn back...

Naveena Bhashini

THANK YOU...!

Naveena Bhashini

~End~

Connect with the Author

Instagram:
its_bhashy_here

Naveena Bhashini

www.noellorenz.com

Naveena Bhashini

www.ingramcontent.com/pod-product-compliance
Lightning Source LLC
Chambersburg PA
CBHW061334120726
48001CB00002B/853